TOUGH LESSONS

Flight Nurse Learned
How to Manage Turbulence in the Air
and in Her Life, and You Can Too!

MARY HART

POWERED BY
black card
BOOKS

Author: Mary Hart
Title: Tough Lessons
ISBN: 978-1-77204-053-1
Category: SELF-HELP/Personal Growth/Success

Publisher:
Black Card Books
Division of Gerry Robert Enterprises Inc.
Suite 214, 5-18 Ringwood Drive
Stouffville, Ontario
Canada, L4A 0N2
International Calling: 1 647 361 8577
www.blackcardbooks.com

TOUGH LESSONS

Flight Nurse Learned
How to Manage Turbulence in the Air
and in Her Life, and You Can Too!

Dan—
I did it! Best to you

MARY HART

Mary Hart

POWERED BY

black card
B O O K S

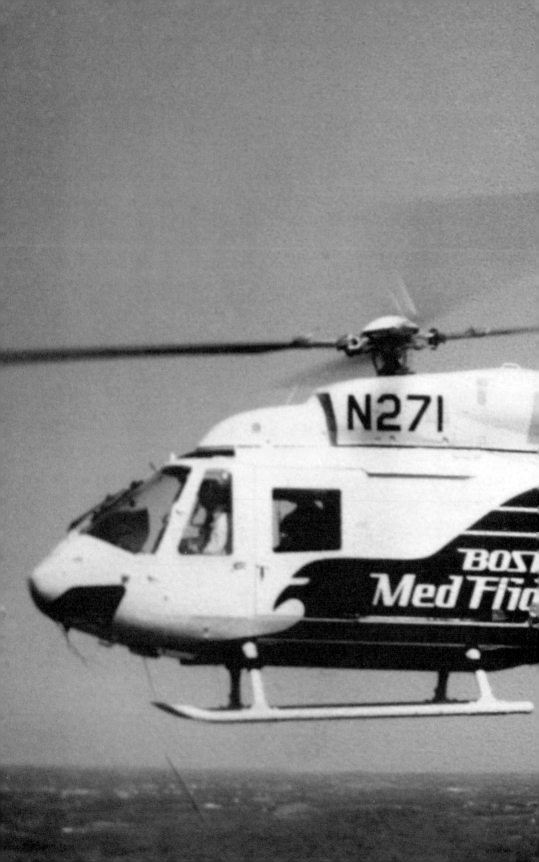

Table of Contents

Endorsement

"Mary's journey, as told through the words of her powerful book, is inspiring, enlightening, and motivating! The experiences she encountered in her life, and the invaluable lessons she derived from them, will assist you on your own journey of personal empowerment!"

Sherry Brantley
Bestselling author of *STEPP (Start To Exercise Personal Power): How To Create Positive Change In Your Life!*
www.steppbook.com

>>>>>>>>>>>>>>>>>>>>>>>>>>>>>>>>>>>>>>

Acknowledgements

Thank you, Gerry Robert, for all your support and guidance, and the support of Black Card Books during the writing of this book. Through some health crisis during the time of this writing, everyone demonstrated utmost support and patience as I worked my way through the process.

A special thanks to Leilani, my niece, who devoted some time to review my manuscript.

Dedication

This book is dedicated to my parents and siblings, without whom I would not be who I am today.

Preface

L ike a lot of people, I wanted to write a book. As a registered nurse, the idea for the subject of the book varied, from how to skillfully insert a peripheral intravenous catheter, to my experience while undergoing chemotherapy, to why retire. When my writing coach, Wendy Gallagher, learned of my subject ideas, her advice was immediate. Write about my nursing career as a flight nurse.

Half Chinese, one-eighth Native American, and a mix of Caucasian blood, I grew up during an era of discrimination. The loss of our mother at an early age placed a burden of responsibilities on our father, with six children under the age of 11. All six children in our family grew out of poverty and went on to have successful careers and lives.

My life is about making choices and taking advantage of opportunities that came my way. This book is for individuals who think they have less. How one can, by choice and actions, grow into the person they want to be. I hope you enjoy the recounting of my journey as I crossed the country as a flight nurse and helped develop some of the first medical emergency helicopter transport programs in the U.S. This book is not a confession or biography. My goal is to inspire you to reach for your goals despite your circumstances. It takes action on your part and the support of great individuals around you. My heartfelt thanks to the great staff support at Black Card Books.

Chapter 1

GROWING UP POOR

"Don't confuse your path with your destination.
Just because it's stormy now doesn't mean that you
aren't headed for sunshine. – Unknown"

Growing Up

The doctor had not arrived at the hospital, thus nurses sedated my mother to slow my birth. Do you suppose that was my first experience with impatience and frustration? I was born December 26 just after midnight, the second of six children born to Ray L. Hart and Elsie K. Y. Wong Hart of Rural Route, Carson City, Michigan.

A U.S. Army soldier, Dad met Mom while stationed in Hawaii during World War II. He was obnoxious when they first met and she threw a pair of scissors at him. Love prevailed and they were married in Hawaii and went on to have six children. My siblings' names in order of birth as they are referenced later on: Betty, Mary, Ray Jr. (Junior), Beta, Judy, and Joe.

Dad said, "Maybe we should have stayed in Hawaii. Mom never became pregnant while there." There is some truth to that, given the temperature differences between Hawaii and Michigan. Lucky for us, Michigan was home.

Mom was the second oldest of seven siblings and cared for her younger siblings after the death of their mother. With this responsibility, she managed to finish high school.

On the other hand, Dad went to work after eighth grade to help feed his family of four siblings and his parents.

He worked in the Civilian Conservation Camps (CCC) in the Upper Peninsula of Michigan. The CCC provided work constructing improvements to park systems during the depression. A large portion of wages, of less than $30 per month, was sent home to support families.

We grew up on a 65-acre farm southeast of Carson City. The land was productive, used for growing crops of corn, wheat, oats, and beans. Mom and Dad tended a food garden and raised pigs and chickens.

Dad would fish and hunt game animals. There were hunting seasons for deer, pheasants, ducks, quails, squirrels, and rabbits. Fishing caught walleye, bluegill, perch, pike, smelt, and suckers. Garden produce was canned.

Meats from hunting and fishing were stored frozen in a rented freezer locker at the store in town. Refrigerator freezers of the '50s could only hold a half gallon of soft ice cream. We even had frog legs and snapping turtles. During spring, we would hunt for morel mushrooms, a favorite treat.

A meal of these foods today requires a trip to a gourmet restaurant.

Mom taught us to sew on a treadle sewing machine. The machine, operated by my feet, was powerful as I once sewed through my finger. It was almost as traumatic as running my arm into the wringer on the washing machine up to the elbow before I could hit the release! She also taught me embroidery stitches for a small table runner. All these skills would become very important in 1958.

We didn't have much money, therefore no luxuries or store-bought toys. Our farm was our playground. The buildings and trees were our jungle gyms. We had a daring plan to harness Judy in ropes so we could pull her over the roof of the barn—luckily, this plan was abandoned. We went wading in the drainage ditch, caught small critters, and got cut up by cut grass. We picked wild berries and apples that grew along the roadside. We entered the well frequently to prime the water pump, always careful not to slip or fall into the narrow water pipe below the pump. Luckily, we did not suffer any major injuries.

At an early age we learned to tend the garden and can the food using a pressure cooker or water bath. Each summer, the pantry was

filled with home-canned goods. Cabbage, carrots, pumpkins, and potatoes were stored in the cellar for winter use. Sauerkraut was placed in the basement for a dark cool area in which to cure. Tamping cabbage with salt into jars until the juices flowed was a satisfying activity. According to Grandma Hart, it should be made at a certain point in the moon cycle to prevent the jars from exploding—I didn't know when, we'd always just ask her if it was time.

It was now 1957 and tens of thousands of people were dying in the pandemic swine flu outbreak. My mother was one of its victims in December of that year.

My last memory of her etched in my mind is of her lying in bed when she asked if I wanted her to die. As a lump formed in my throat and tears welled in my eyes, I turned away so she couldn't see me cry. I could not answer. I wished I had said no but I did not have the courage to answer. The question was not a usual question from mother to daughter, of which there can be no explanation.

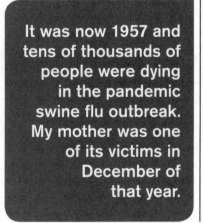

It was now 1957 and tens of thousands of people were dying in the pandemic swine flu outbreak. My mother was one of its victims in December of that year.

Mom was too young to die at the tender age of 33. Dad, only five years older, now had the sole responsibility to care for six children. This, no doubt, was a tremendous strain for him. Though he managed to keep us together, he smoked and drank too much alcohol. The smoking would lead to severe emphysema and ultimately be the reason for his death at age 61 due to respiratory failure.

Discrimination

Mom never had an easy life. Of Chinese descent, she was born and raised in Hawaii. In Michigan, she was not met with open arms. It was the '40s and '50s. Not until the Civil Rights Act of 1964 was discrimination based on race, color, religion, sex, or national origin outlawed. Discrimination existed throughout the country. As we grew up, we felt the discrimination. Our Chinese mother was not welcomed, not only by townspeople but by relatives, since they equated her race and national origin as "chink". Fresh on the minds of many was WWII against the Japanese.

"Chink" was just one of the name-calling labels we experienced. Dad, of Native American descent, passed on his ability to tan to a deep brown down to his children. Since we played outside and enjoyed outdoor activities all summer, we would tan to a dark brown color. The darkened skin invited taunts of "nigger" from peers. The father of my sister's friend asked her to leave their home because of her race. Another sister avoided the sun to keep her skin pale. Imagine our empathy when a black family moved to the community. And then another. That made a total of four families of color, including a Mexican family, whose father worked on a local farm. I'm sure they all were taunted and pressured because of their color as I was. This was the reason Betty finished college and moved to Hawaii where she could be in the majority race.

Mom had one friend, Grandma Patton, our next-door neighbor. She was not related but a kind individual who supported our family. She befriended Mom, provided her transportation and helped by making our school dresses.

One day, my oldest sister Betty was swinging on a rope hung from the barn rafters. Her foot broke through a window pane and severed her Achilles' tendon. With fear and dread in my mind, I ran to Grandma Patton's to get help. Mom, who didn't drive, got the old Ford car started and was able to drive Betty to the Patton's, arriving at almost the same time as I did. The things one can do should the need arise.

Grandma Patton drove them to the doctor. Betty returned after a hospital stay with a heavy toe-to-thigh plaster cast. She was ordered to stay in a chair. One evening, I tried to help lift the cast so she could move to look outside. The cast was so heavy I dropped her leg. It was a painful experience for her. How she was able to move with that heavy cast is a mystery. I do not recall trying to move her again.

An occasional Sunday trip to Grandma Hart's and even rarer trip to Uncle Ben's was the extent of our family travel. From Grandma's, we would go to the river for a picnic lunch, to fish and play on the river bank. If we were lucky, we could go out on the river in the fishing boat. The grown-up men would be out on the river in the small fishing boat trolling for walleye all day.

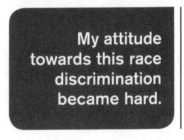

My attitude towards this race discrimination became hard.

Uncle Tim, Mom's brother, was our most notable visitor. He was in the military and came to see her one summer. He instructed us to help Mom clean the house. She must have been very busy, tending to six children, with all the laundry, gardening and preserving of foods she accomplished. I don't know how much of help we were. I only have snippets of memories before age eight. Memories relate to my learning a task such as sewing. It was a time of endless summers, especially notable after the start of school. I remember when I would lie spread-eagled on the lawn after spinning around until dizziness caused me to fall; the movement of clouds was the earth moving.

One night while we slept, our mother was taken by an ambulance to the hospital and died. Although the Carson City Hospital was less than three miles away, she was transported to St. John's Hospital nearly 28 miles away. Rumor had it she was refused admittance to the Carson Hospital because of her race. Dad had Grandma Patton come to our house to announce to us that Mom had died. I was sitting with my feet on the apron of the heating stove for warmth when she delivered the news.

My attitude towards this race discrimination became hard. If people didn't like me because of my ethnicity, it didn't matter; I learned to shut people out. I was content with a small circle of friends. I learned to be self-reliant. Betty had the responsibility of cooking and I did the dishes. We all shared the responsibilities for cleaning, laundry, gardening, and attending school. We raised each other.

> In the spring following Mom's passing, the house burned.

Unfortunate Event

In the spring following Mom's passing, the house burned. The firemen thought that it was caused by children playing with matches. I admit to playing with matches but not setting fires. Before Mom died, the three of us oldest siblings stole Dad's cigarettes and practiced smoking in the granary and in our upstairs room. We hid the butts and spent matches behind a bedroom chest.

Mom had found the cigarette stash and gathered us together. She had an offer. We could continue to smoke. They would provide us with the cigarettes if we smoked in front of them. She held out the package offering a cigarette. Despite Betty and Junior's encouragement and praise of my expertise at smoking, I refused. Mom used reverse psychology to get us to stop smoking— and if that was her plan, it worked. None of the three of us ever smoked as an adult.

No one was playing with matches at the time of the fire. It was after school and some of us were watching TV and some were outside playing. Firemen found a stash of matches in my brother's toy truck, which led them to their conclusion. In reality, it was clothing that was too close to the stove pipe in the upper floor that started the fire. The coal stove pipe that extended up through a grate in the floor to the roof chimney got hot. We kids didn't keep a neat house. We played with matches while up under the crawl space of the house. Candles made from string and paraffin wax were best demonstrated there because it was dark!

The great old two-storey farmhouse was cut down to one level. Dad, with the help of Grandpa Hart, rebuilt it into a three-bedroom house. The one-storey wing at the back of the house, a bedroom, and the pantry were salvaged. During the reconstruction was being done, we lived in an old silver-colored school bus, fitted for use as a hunting camper. Behind the driver seat was a couch, to the left was a kerosene space heater, a table, and a two-burner propane cooktop. We slept in the back on mattresses on the floor.

Once the house was finished, we had bedrooms. The house had running water in the kitchen but no indoor bathroom or toilet.

With six of us taking a bath in the same tub water once a week, I tried to be first. The rickety outhouse, a dark and spooky space at night, cold during winter, a fly magnet in the summer, and often without toilet paper, was still needed. Two things that have remained with me to this day:

1. I never ever run out of toilet paper!
2. I don't like camping!

We constructed stick play horses out of the wood lath ripped from the old house. I hinged the neck on mine so I could rein it in. We would play workup baseball every night after school during the summer; playing outfield, pitcher, batter, then catcher. I was at bat. Following through on a mighty "swing and a miss", I hit Junior on the temple. He dropped like a sack of potatoes. I feared I had killed him, as Dad had always warned us: "Do not hit anyone in the temple because you could kill them."

I didn't knock any sense into Junior or cause a head bleed.

That summer, I won a three-speed bicycle from the drugstore contest. A girl had given me all her points so I could win. This was my first experience with an act of kindness from an unidentified stranger. We all learned to ride on that bicycle. It was used to travel down to the creek when we went fishing. Sometimes, we went spearing at night. Dad would wade the creek carrying a lantern for light to see the fish. Once he speared one, he would throw it to the bank. We would run along the dark landscape to bag and carry it. In the early evening, we would pick up night crawlers to use for fishing bait. Have you ever pounced on a night crawler, grasped it and have it elongate twice its length as you pulled? This required mental preparation before the first crawler was captured. We spent a lot of time outdoors being active playing, as well as completing farm chores. One chore was to pull weeds from fields of beans after school.

We would make a game of it, racing to the end and back to reward ourselves with a drink of Kool-Aid.

At night and evenings, we could tune in stations from far away on our old radio... WBZ Boston, WLS Chicago, and the Grand Ole Opry WSM Nashville. A station would broadcast "Hawaii Calls" from Hawaii. Dad loved to listen. He always wanted to revisit Hawaii but was never able to do so. Sitting, with my head pressed to the radio, I listened to Superman, Paladin, Johnny Dollar, and the Lone Ranger. A fan of the Detroit Tigers, we would listen to the game play-by-play by Ernie Harwell.

Dad obtained employment at the telephone company to support us. Each summer was a lesson in "there is no money, I'm not made of money, I can't afford that," when we would present our Sears order for school clothes for Dad to send a check. We'd show Dad the order—underwear, clothing and shoes for everyone. The initial order, often $100, would be rejected. We'd examine the catalog to find cheaper products until the order was $50 or less, then Dad sent the order. Instead of buying ready-made clothes, we ordered less expensive fabric and made some of our own clothing.

Revising our order down in dollar value drove home the idea of scarcity of money.

Revising our order down in dollar value drove home the idea of scarcity of money. This idea of scarcity persisted in my mind even when I made good money later in life. A feeling that I didn't have any money even with a substantial bank balance always persisted. I'm getting over that limiting idea. When we got lucky, someone would drop off used clothing and we found something that fit. I wore second-hand shoes to school one day and after laughter at my shoes embarrassed me to tears, I walked home. Dad was there. I told him my story and went to bed crying. God bless The Salvation Army, as they would come by on Thanksgiving or Christmas and give us a turkey.

During the summers of the high school years, we worked jobs. I sorted and bagged potatoes in a potato factory and worked as a nurse's aide at the small city hospital. My assigned areas were the

> Growing up
> with scarcity,
> poverty and
> discrimination,
> I hoped getting
> an education
> would lead to
> something better.

post-partum obstetrics, delivery room, and nursery. I would bathe and dress newborns in their first clothing. One night an older licensed practical nurse fell asleep while sitting in a rocking chair in the nursery. When she was fired for this, it disturbed me greatly. Crying, I asked Dad why people were so cruel. What would become of the poor, old woman? He had no answer.

The End of Childhood

I graduated high school with honors in the class' top 10.

During senior year, aptitude tests determined our talents. A high score in biology pointed me to the field of medicine. The decision was made to go to college. Growing up with scarcity, poverty and discrimination, I hoped getting an education would lead to something better. I wanted nice housing (with indoor plumbing), to travel, and have money. Betty and I sought higher education; our other siblings became successful by experience.

At the time, I didn't have any money or thoughts on how to get it. I had a goal.

Lessons to Take Away from This Chapter:

1. Poverty in your past is no reason to live poor forever.
2. Middle school taunts can make you grow, and they do come to an end.
3. If you want change, set a goal and make a decision, and take action to reach your goal.

*"The ultimate reason for setting goals is to entice you
to become the person it takes to achieve them."*
—*Jim Rohn*

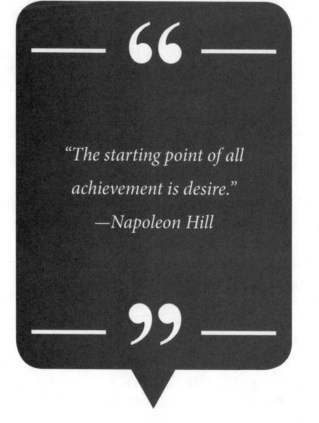

"*The starting point of all achievement is desire.*"
—*Napoleon Hill*

Chapter 2

I FOUND THE MONEY

College Days

My interest was in art. I could draw a little, knit, embroider, and sew clothes. After a review with advisors during my senior year, a life as a starving artist was not attractive. Remember, I wanted indoor plumbing. So nursing school it was. Both the Michigan State University (MSU) and the University of Michigan (UM) nursing school accepted my applications. Because Betty was already attending MSU, I decided that getting a ride to MSU in East Lansing might be easier than getting to UM in Ann Arbor, and therefore chose MSU. A decision of practicality. Betty pointed out that rarely did we ever travel together but that was the rationale.

Tuition was covered by scholarships, loans, and Dad. Working in the cafeteria and library helped pay for clothes, food, and books. After living in the dormitory for a year, there came the opportunity to live in a house off-campus. This was a new experience. Accommodating others by leaving the shower selector on the tub in the off position was a learned skill.

Classes went well enough. The speaking skills of the professors became a strong influence on my final grade. One professor said "ah" very frequently. Class became a game of "ah" counting sessions. What a distraction. Had I known, I could have directed him to Toastmasters. One of the duties in Toastmasters is to be an "ah" counter. (On a personal note, I am a member of Toastmasters. It's a great non-threatening place to hone speaking skills.)

The first two years at university weeded out many students who started with a nursing major. The School of Nursing's goal was to teach us foundational principles since we could not experience everything in clinical rotations. We could apply the principles to function in any situation. A Bachelor of Science Degree in Nursing was being promoted as the preferred nurse education. It seemed best to start with a bachelor's degree, though nursing salaries did not reflect any difference in pay or responsibility for diploma, associate degree, or BSN nurses.

> The School of Nursing's goal was to teach us foundational principles since we could not experience everything in clinical rotations.

In junior year, the military came to recruit nurses. There were two options to join the military for tuition assistance: One year of tuition assistance mandated two years active duty; two years of tuition assistance required three years of active duty. I needed a car in senior year to get to clinical class sites each semester. Mental health training required a commute to Pontiac, Michigan, and medical-surgical rotations were at hospitals in the Lansing metropolitan area. After looking at the Navy, Air Force, and Army, I enlisted in the Army. The small enlistee salary made me rich.

My tuition was paid and I had enough money to buy a car: A Ford Cortina with a four-cylinder engine and manual transmission. It was so light that getting stuck during the winter was no problem. With the car in first gear, the tires spinning, I got out to push it and once it got traction, I jumped in and took off.

I didn't develop a preference for a specialty nursing practice but knew what I did not like—public health or psychiatric nursing. Public health, since I felt that you could not change how people lived, and psych patients, I thought, were just crazy. The personality, skills, experience, and interests of an individual lead them to choose a particular area of clinical nursing practice.

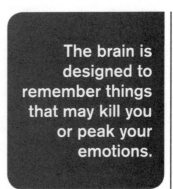

The brain is designed to remember things that may kill you or peak your emotions.

In my last year at MSU, a breast biopsy of a mass was benign, thankfully. Shortly thereafter, I was diagnosed with mononucleosis. I had to refrain from working as a graduate nurse.

After passing my nursing boards at the first take, I became a licensed Registered Nurse. That fall, I drove in a new car to San Antonio, Texas for Officer Training School. Training must not have been very intense because I remember little of it. The brain is designed to remember things that may kill you or peak your emotions. Where were you on Sept. 11, 2011?

My three preferences for duty stations were Denver, Seattle, and San Diego. My first duty station was at Fort Gordon Army Hospital (now Dwight David Eisenhower Army Medical Center) in

Augusta, Georgia. So much for preferences. My little sister Beta flew to Texas to accompany me back to Michigan before I drove to GA. We enjoyed driving fast my new car: A 1970 red Camaro—350 engine, 250 horsepower, with four on the floor Hurst shifter. We changed one flat tire without difficulty, independent girls that we were!

Active Military Service

All of my belongings fit in my car's back seat and trunk. I drove cross-country by myself. In Georgia, I roomed with Janet from basic training. My duty was to supervise the surgical wards. Most patients were combat Veterans who returned from Vietnam. Many were leaving the Army after they rehabbed from their wounds.

I received orders for Vietnam (RVN) and Janet, orders for Korea. Jungle gear was issued for me, cold weather gear for Janet.

For the first time, I was witness to the death of a patient. The cancer patient was receiving frequent doses of a narcotic to ease the pain. He died one night after I gave him pain medication. A startling awareness. Did the pain medicine cause death or as intended—help comfort him at the end of his time? This was one of many firsts for me. The first shot I ever gave was to a child in the anterior left thigh. I swore I felt the parting of the muscle fibers by the needle! After a startle, oh how he cried! I remember turning off blood pressure support medications to brain-dead patients. One woman lasted the exact number of minutes equal to the years she had been married to the husband who waited at her bedside. Peak emotional experiences created these memories. One is torn sometimes. These orders to cease measures that keep a body alive are always based on clinical evidence. It requires practice of disinterest—meaning one cannot allow personal emotion to affect decisions.

Thinking Janet and I would continue at Fort Gordon another year, we started making plans to go to Orlando, Florida the next year to attend the opening of Disney World. We had explored the area, made short trips to Florida's Daytona Beach and Tampa, Florida visiting crocodile farms and other attractions. I received orders for Vietnam (RVN) and Janet, orders for Korea. Jungle gear was issued for me, cold weather gear for Janet. The only way to get out of this undesired order was to get court-martialed, go to Canada, or get pregnant. None seemed a realistic option so we followed orders.

My rank was now 1st Lieutenant, soon to be Captain as I prepared to participate in this unpopular war. Actress Jane Fonda, outspoken in her lack of support for the war effort, visited Hanoi in July of 1972 while I toured Vietnam. Her actions created hostility. Anti-war sentiment was high; soldiers returning home received no welcome. Draft dodgers were escaping to Canada.

My belongings and my car were left with Beta in Michigan with instructions not to let little Joe drive the car. On the west coast, I boarded an airplane and headed halfway around the world. During the descent to Guam, pressure in my left ear did not equalize. It caused a most excruciating pain in my ear. The flight attendants placed a heated cup over my ear and encouraged me to take in a deep breath, plug my nose and bear down to force air into the tubes leading to the ears to break the blockage. This effort intensified the pain. After what seemed like an eternity, with painful effort in an airplane at a Guam airport, I was able to break open my ear canal.

Vietnam

Once we touched down in RVN, the first thing I noted was that the air smelled bad. They said it was a result of the lack of sanitation. Off the commercial aircraft, we flew in utility military transport planes.

Ground transport by bus was driven under a yellow caution to the base for processing in-country. Halted a couple of times, everyone maintained complete silence awaiting word to proceed. Never was there a quieter, subdued group of young adults on a bus.

Pat, a roommate from basic training, was my RVN roommate. My assignment was the emergency room at the 67th Evac Hospital, Qui Nhon. The hospital was a complex of wooden barracks, quonset huts, and some concrete structures located next to the flight line of an airfield. The year was 1971. The bloody battles with mass casualties of war were essentially over. Small incidents brought occasional casualties to We reviewed the logs to see the large numbers and the severe injuries of those wounded in the Tet Offensive of '68. The image of the charred body of a soldier burned to death at a battle shortly after my arrival at Qui Nhon is still etched in my mind to this day.

On New Year's night, while working the night shift, we witnessed tracer rounds shot across our front door area. Cheap, deadly fireworks. We stayed inside.

Many nurses and doctors never wished to be in Vietnam. Alcohol and marijuana were in high use. Some got into heroin although they continually denied that they were using. "Must be lab error," they said in response to positive urine drug screens. Many painful penicillin shots were given for gonorrhea. I, on the other hand, trained in Tae Kwon Do, lessons given by a Korean soldier. I never once thought that drugs were the answer to my situation.

To benefit local people, we would go on dental and medical missions to pull teeth and provide basic medical care to poverty-stricken Vietnamese. One place we went to was a leprosarium run by French nuns. The beach where they lived was well-known for its undercurrent and several people had died in the South China Sea at this location.

The food at the leprosarium was amazing! Nuns served several course meals of fine French-prepared food and homemade wine. A little bit of luxury at a leprosarium in a war zone.

To break up the serious nature of our work, the medical staff planned a New Year's Day football game. It would be men versus women, the Chickens versus Rita's Warriors. Good-natured memos passed back and forth. Effigies of chickens were hung by the neck. Game day came complete with a float. The men used up all the toilet paper, secretly making a big chicken float mounted on a jeep.

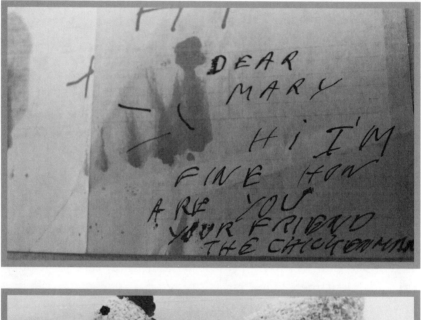

It was the first and last Bush Bowl super bowl at the 67th Evac Hospital, Qui Nhon in 1972. The women lost. The 67th hospital was closed down after the New Year and the area became a camp. I was transferred to the 3rd Field Hospital in Saigon.

Soldiers from the combat areas would come to the officers' club. Their stories were sad. They were so glad to be back to civilization, having a chance to dry out. Up in the jungle near Pleiku, much of the fighting continued in a wet, jungle environment. Their boots wore out and they were unable to get new ones. Socks and poncho liners were not available for them, however Saigon street vendors had all these items. That really angered me. The presence of these items on the street display indicated they had a source that the soldiers did not.

When the police thought I was a Vietnamese woman with army soldiers, I was stopped on the street. Luckily, my ID ended the stop without incident.

Vietnam came with an opportunity. One day, a couple of soldiers proposed an idea to me. Stereo, TV, jewelry, and money were mine if only I would work in a bar and talk to customers. Really? Talk? I declined since it seemed there might be more involved than conversation. And was it even legal?

The most disappointing incident occurred one day when we were told to prepare for casualties from an offensive operation about to begin. As head of the emergency room, I was in charge of getting the ER ready for incoming casualties. We had no chest X-ray film! Only small films to X-ray a hand or foot were available. There was no way to X-ray a chest or abdomen, which are the first films needed in trauma assessment. Angry, I marched to the head of the Nursing Corps and ranted about how negligent this was, especially since the reason there was no film was that the supply personnel had sold the film on the black market. That, along with soldiers not having new boots, poncho liners, or socks, were unforgivable offenses. We were lucky that casualties did not come in as the conflict was averted. War is hell.

R&R, rest and recovery time, was spent in Taipei, Taiwan, Hong Kong and Bangkok, Thailand. Most notable was the smell of Taipei as it was fresh and clean. These were great places to visit to experience the culture and see the sites in these countries. The familiar bad smell greeted me upon returning to Vietnam.

When my time became short, less than 30 days left to go in-country, I received a seven-day drop. I was going home a week early! Upon arrival, after I stepped out of the airplane on the west coast, I did what many did: I kissed the ground. While in Vietnam, we missed freedom: Freedom to go to McDonald's or a supermarket to get whatever we wanted. The liberties we have in the United States are unmatched anywhere in the world, no matter how irritated we are with politics. The fact that in Vietnam we slept with a rifle, ammo, a flak jacket, and helmet under the bed was never mentioned. We were fighting a war that was not a war. Few wanted to be there, from government officials down to the soldiers in the field. No one welcomed us home at the airfield. I never voluntarily spoke about being in Vietnam for many, many years.

> Upon arrival, after I stepped out of the airplane on the west coast, I did what many did: I kissed the ground.

A job at Denver General Hospital (now Denver Health Medical Center) emergency room was my goal after heading home to Michigan. I paid off my car and student loans, packed up and headed for Colorado. Three of my siblings had gotten married and each had toddlers to raise. My older sister and youngest brother and I were unattached. Little Joe won all the quarter-mile drag races with my Camaro. Glad to be back on U.S. soil, I was on the road again.

State Side: Denver, Colorado

I moved in with Pat from Qui Nhon. There were no job openings at Denver General, thus I worked at the University Hospital. A general surgery, genital-urinary, and eye surgical unit was my first place of work. This was not my cup of tea. One morning, I missed giving the "every-five-minute" eye drops for an eye surgery. Upset, frustrated, I quit and went to the Veterans Administration Hospital (VA) next door to work in the intensive care unit. Being a nurse turned out to be a good choice of profession since there were several job openings from which to choose.

> Intensive care nursing, care of the critically ill, I liked.

Intensive care nursing, care of the critically ill, I liked. Much of my time was in the isolation intensive care, which housed sick patients who had developed sepsis or wound infections. We rushed one patient down the hall on more than one occasion, riding his

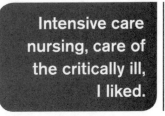

bed to surgery to hold pressure and stop his bleeding. Each time we thought it might be his last trip. When he was stable, we would look at brochures of the truck that he wished to buy when he was able to go home. Open-heart surgeries were being pioneered. In-depth knowledge of intensive care became part of my nursing identity.

A lesson in documentation: A few years later, I received a call from an investigator for a pending case. The patient was suing the VA for having lost sight in his eye. He was a somewhat crusty, elderly man who would refuse to let us put in his eye drops. This I had documented in his patient record, thus he did not have facts to substantiate his claim of neglect. Accurate documentation is so important.

Promotion to a head nurse position of a surgical floor came after one year. I moved into my own apartment and shopped for a house. After six months, I went hunting for a job in the emergency room at St. Anthony's Hospital.

Lessons to Take Away from This Chapter:

1. War is hell. It causes high mental stress, especially when it does not meet with the approval of the world.
2. There is no place like the United States.
3. It may take a while to find your niche… don't settle for less.

~∞∞∞~

"Always remember that your present situation is not your final destination. The best is yet to come."
— *Zig Ziglar*

~∞∞∞~

Get a FREE Perspective Dialogue
with Mary Hart. Scan this code
and click info@toughlessons.net
to send an email.

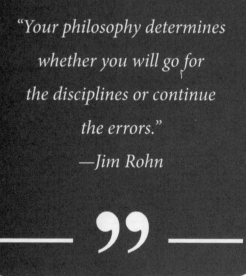

"Your philosophy determines
whether you will go for
the disciplines or continue
the errors."
—Jim Rohn

Chapter 3

FLIGHT NURSING

Emergency Medicine

While waiting for my interview at St. Anthony's, a woman walked in and announced, "We're opening some positions in the flight program." She looked at me. "You qualify. Would you like to be a flight nurse?" She was an administrator of the Flight for Life program. In the right place at the right time, I said yes to the opportunity.

The program drew from experiences treating casualties in the Korean and Vietnam wars. Unfortunate as war is, advances in medical and trauma care have been expedited through observations by medical professionals during wars and applied to civilian medicine. Historically, it began with the tourniquet, blood transfusions, penicillin, mobile field hospitals with trained field

medical personnel, helicopter transport, paramedics, and helicopter transport. Civilian medical doctors recognized that the critically injured from motor vehicle crashes, wounded from gunshots, knives, assaults by fists, or blunt weapons were similar to the war injured, and could benefit from quick intervention to improve the quality of the outcome.

M*A*S*H, the TV program, demonstrated how injured patients were evacuated in a rescue basket hanging from a helicopter in Korea. Vietnam missions were more sophisticated. Patients were transported

inside Huey helicopters. Interventions were implemented as soon as possible after the injury by medical personnel on the ground. Patients were then taken to strategically-located hospital facilities.

The civilian concept of implementing care and helicopter transport in the "Golden Hour", the period of 60 minutes or less following an injury, was begun by Dr. R. Adams Cowley in Maryland. He, along with the Maryland State Police Aviation Division, developed a statewide emergency medical service to transport trauma victims to Shock Trauma Centers by helicopter.

Physicians at St. Anthony's Hospital recognized the "Golden Hour" significance. Their unique idea was to crew with a registered nurse, trained to physician-level skill and knowledge, to care for critically ill and injured patients from scenes of accidents or between hospital facilities, while being transported in a helicopter or fixed-wing aircraft.

The concept of the Level I trauma teams was spreading throughout the country. Level I Trauma Centers had highly skilled specialists in-house. Centers were capable of responding to any type of emergency with the appropriate specialist.

Trauma team roles were divided and tasks and procedures were assigned to a specific individual. When the patient arrived, each individual carried out their assigned task almost simultaneously.

Patients were efficiently assessed, scanned, X-rayed, had their blood work done, and were in operating rooms within minutes after arrival. A skilled trauma team in action is a choreographed, efficient team effort. Similar protocols were developed for medical emergencies.

The flight nurse training class began with three nurses. Training centered on aircraft safety, flight physiology, stresses of flight, emergency medicine, trauma and medical emergencies. The pilots were responsible for the aircraft and flying. The crew had to be aware of the basics of weight and balance. Roundtrip fuel needs were critical. Landing sites on the streets or remote areas did not have fuel stations or trucks. Fueling the aircraft with passengers aboard was not permitted for safety reasons.

Takeoff and landing an aircraft is the most potentially dangerous time of flight. Autorotation was practiced. Helicopters rarely land at approved sights when picking up accident victims. Flashlights, lanterns, car and emergency vehicle lights were often the best lights at night. Streets, fields, clearings in the woods, wherever the helicopter could be positioned safely in a 60x60 feet unobstructed area to land near the patient's location were used. For medical missions, pilots often have to land fixed-wing craft on unimproved airstrips that are packed dirt or sometimes grass, and have no towers, or no landing lights.

We communicated to each other by headset over the radio to base or the intercom system. The nurse provided extra eyes looking out for obstacles and ensuring the clearance of the tail rotor during landings and takeoffs. We would open the door and stick our heads out to look for obstructions near the tail rotor. Though I have a fear of heights, not once did I experience fear in the helicopter or fixed-wing aircraft. Rooftop helipads required acclimatization.

The usual flight crew consisted of one pilot and one nurse. A helicopter was stationed at St. Anthony's Central and one at St. Anthony's North with two fixed-wing aircraft at Stapleton Airport. Nurses rotated between locations and duty on helicopter or fixed-wing missions. In the case of multiple patients at incidents, both helicopters could respond.

The flight nurse training course lasted several weeks. In addition to lectures, there were skill labs to learn techniques such as endotracheal intubation, emergency tracheostomy, insertion of intravenous catheters (peripheral and central lines), and needling of the chest to release air, to name a few. We also attended the Advanced Trauma Life Support Class. We were certified as Critical Care Practitioners as approved by the Colorado American College of Surgeons upon completion of training.

The aircraft was stocked with oxygen and all the resuscitative equipment and medications for emergencies. At the start of the shift and after every flight, the helicopter equipment was checked, restocked, and readied for the next flight. Getting to the scene of an accident without needed equipment or medicine could only be the fault of the nurse on duty. We did have a couple of great tech experts who did a lot of equipment upkeep, but it was ultimately each nurse's responsibility.

I learned much even when not on flights. As a resource for the hospital units, we were called to start difficult intravenous (IV) lines, draw blood gas samples, or place an airway tube in cardiac arrest patients. After enduring numerous needle stick attempts and misses to obtain blood or start an intravenous line by another nurse, the patient would allow me one chance to start the IV or draw a blood gas sample. My skills improved continuously by doing the most difficult blood draw or IV start. We improved and maintained our intubation skill (placing airway tubes) by intubating patients in the operating room. Working at the emergency department (ER)

exposed us to the many types of patients who were admitted with a medical emergency. By observing patients as they entered the door, we would assess the way they walked and held themselves to conclude if they were sick or not and what was the most likely complaint. Not all people who present themselves at the emergency room have an emergency. Shocking, I know. We would check to see if our assessment was correct. Close observation can reveal a lot about a chief complaint. I was very proud one day when I recognized a case of malaria. And yes, this assessment was confirmed after just a verbal interview.

Each week, missions were reviewed in the flight crew meeting. A nurse would recount a mission and the medical director would critique if the case was a demonstration of proper medical care or, if not, make recommendations on how it could have been handled better. We saw some rare diseases we would never have seen in routine nursing positions. It was a great learning environment. As a quote from Jim Rohn goes, "You are the average of the five people you spend most time with." This being the case, among a ground-breaking group of medical experts, I was at the most knowledgeable time in my career. It was a great place to be.

> **Not all people who present themselves at the emergency room have an emergency. Shocking, I know.**

Lessons of a New Flight Nurse

I learned a huge life lesson after being on an aircraft whose engine failed while a patient was in my care. The patient, with a possible head injury, was being transferred from the Steamboat Springs Clinic to Denver for scans not available at the clinic. He was stable and not exhibiting any concerning symptoms. We were aboard a small twin-engine aircraft. Our speed down the runway suddenly

> **Stand up and tell the group why you abandoned your patient.**

diminished as the pilot slowed the aircraft and taxied back to the hangar. He indicated that one of the engines had lost power and would need to be fixed prior to any further attempts at taking off.

The Steamboat Springs airport had a short runway at an altitude of 6,882 feet. Only small aircraft or ones with the capability for short takeoff and landings were allowed in this airport. Emergency landing sites near this airport were not an option.

Being new, I asked my pilot for advice on what to do. He suggested that I return the patient to the clinic and come back to the airport and stay with the aircraft. I followed his advice, never thinking of calling dispatch. The patient was returned to the clinic. He was stable and had not exhibited any signs of bleeding in the brain or increased pressure on the brain. The engine repair took a long time and we returned to Denver late that night.

The next morning, first item on the agenda: The medical director inquired if I was present. "Stand up and tell the group why you abandoned your patient," he instructed.

Embarrassed, I told my story and then he spoke. The clinic had called for a ground ambulance to take the patient to Denver after they found him in the hall unattended for some time. I had assumed, you know "ass of u and me", he was under care. The director suggested a call to dispatch could have arranged ground transport for me to carry out the transfer. Luckily, the patient did not have a severe head injury or bleeding, and did not suffer any problems during transport and was later discharged after scanning.

I was lucky as was the patient. After this incident, any patient in my care would reach the final destination by whatever means necessary. Calling for advice to a higher authority can lead to different decisions. The pilot was not a medical person, his advice was that of a pilot.

Many of the flight nurses expressed relief that they had not been on that flight because they would have done the same. None of us liked being put on the spot during the flight meetings but we all eventually had a turn in the hot seat. This was tough at the time but we increased our knowledge by reviewing flight records and considering alternatives. We learned to respond better rather than react. We learned from others' choices, mistakes, and advice.

It was the middle of the night. Snoozing in the back of the fixed-wing aircraft, I awoke as the pilot began making low passes over the field in which the runway was located. It was an unlit dirt landing strip in Kansas. Visibility from my seat facing to the rear on the left side of the aircraft was poor. Only dirt ground was visible. The lighting was dim at best. The pilot made his decision and landed. The ground was rough. The ride was bumpy. The nose wheel of the aircraft, caught in soft earth, turned and broke, causing the plane to come to a sudden halt, nose down to the dirt, the left propeller damaged. We had landed in a plowed field adjacent to the hard dirt-packed runway. I left the pilot and broken aircraft with instructions to call me when we had another aircraft.

> **Recognize self-accomplishments when you excel.**

During this mission, I became aware of the confidence Dr. Boyd Bigelow, our pulmonary specialist, expressed in my ability to care for an acutely ill patient. In an "a-ha" moment, I realized that my expertise was recognized by my peers and physician mentors. It was growth in self-confidence, I had developed expertise as a flight nurse. Recognize self-accomplishments when you excel.

Dr. Bigelow's specialty was pulmonary medicine and intensive care. He taught the flight crew frequently. Physician-level content improved the knowledge and skill of the flight crew. He was a mentor to the flight crew and was respected by everyone.

My mission was to transport a patient in cervical traction. He was quadriplegic from a diving incident. It was a fixed-wing flight from New Hampshire to a Denver rehabilitation center. Over New York, one engine failed, requiring an emergency landing. The good news is a twin-engine aircraft can land safely with one functioning engine.

I reverted to safety procedures for the landing. The passenger was strapped into her seat so she was not at risk. The patient and equipment were secured. I did not feel threatened by the emergency landing because my thoughts focused on the safety of the patient or the passenger. My goal was to ensure nothing unfortunate happened to the patient or the passenger. The dispatch center coordinated an ambulance transport and admission of the patient to the nearest hospital for spinal injuries.

This particular flight brought up challenges: Admitting a patient to an unknown hospital out-of-state, and arranging for ambulances with staff abilities to package, repackage, and care for a patient in cervical spinal traction. My job was to supervise the moving, maintenance of the cervical traction, and the positioning of the patient during all the moves. It was necessary to project confidence in an unknown environment. The layover was short. When we returned from dinner, the aircraft was repaired. We packed up and continued our trip without incident to Denver to deliver our patient without any adverse effects.

> Using call sign Life Flight, we had priority when the patient was aboard for takeoff at any airport.

In another incident, we were on the taxiway at a southern Colorado airport heading towards the main runway for takeoff when another plane coming in from the opposite direction, also headed for takeoff, drove right into our left wing. The patient, badly burned in a space heater explosion, was aboard. I was giving intravenous fluids and pain medications. Burn victims require large amounts of fluids in the first few hours. They lose fluids to the weeping of their wounds and swelling, as fluids accumulate in tissues outside the vascular space.

Using call sign Life Flight, we had priority when the patient was aboard for takeoff at any airport. Precious time could be wasted waiting in line on runways with a patient aboard. It was apparent the pilot of the other aircraft was not aware of our status. The impact damaged our left wing and grounded our aircraft. The pilot was one angry and frustrated person as he exited the aircraft to deal with the damages.

An ambulance was summoned to take us back to the hospital from whence we came. It was too far and the patient too critical to go by ground ambulance to Denver. Another aircraft was dispatched to pick us up. When we arrived at the hospital, they were unable to give us a room, indicating they had given over their responsibility to Flight for Life. I asked for any type of room in which I could care for the patient. In an unused X-ray room, I positioned the patient's stretcher on the X-ray table and continued fluid administration.

This was a most frustrating call with one of the most critical patients one can have—severe burns. The sending facility did not want to be helpful and I was very concerned about the patient. My frustration and fear caused me to focus on the infusion of fluids and not registering the adequate urine output. I didn't need to give as much fluid. My focus was narrowed, I was not seeing the big picture. A few deep breaths and recalculation of fluid needs would have been useful.

> Take time to witness the effect of your intervention before you change something. Take a moment to assess what is happening.

Since then I've tried to open my focus to note anything that can affect adjustments or interventional measures in an emergency. This is hard to do. When things are critical, one of the hardest things to do is wait. Take time to witness the effect of your intervention before you change something. Take a moment to assess what is happening.

When the backup aircraft arrived, I was really happy to see that Carol, another flight nurse, had come to help. It was time to place a tube in the patient's airway and she obliged. We made it safely back to Denver with our patient.

The challenges I encountered required decisions to maintain care for patients and deliver them safely to the desired location. The stress of the incidents added to the stress of delivering care to a critical patient. The dispatchers and flight nurses worked as a team to provide the best care and smooth coordination. The dispatch center involved early in a crisis was key. Having flight nurse meetings that regularly reviewed missions and actions constantly expanded knowledge. I learned that I had to remain calm and think through the situations to keep tunnel vision from obscuring the whole picture. Fear, threat, and stress can narrow our focus. Missions improved with awareness because, at first, you don't know what you don't know.

> Fear, threat, and stress can narrow our focus. Missions improved with awareness because, at first, you don't know what you don't know.

In between these flights, I did have routine trauma scene, medical code, neonatal and high-risk pregnancy transfers.

Every flight nurse carried an external brain book. This book contained formulas or information we couldn't keep in our heads. Crew members gave me gifts to insert in my book: Feathers to keep me in the air, a four-leaf clover for luck.

Opportunity Knocking

After three years, hospital Emergency Department Directors and Administrators started visiting St. Anthony's to look at the operation and determine what they needed to do to implement their own programs. A mentor as always, Dr. Bigelow told us, "You all currently have skills no one else has. Your experience is saleable. Now is the time if you want to advance your careers. These people are looking for someone with expertise to guide them in the development of their programs. You want to do it, you need to apply now."

I and several others set off to start new programs. New goal: Implement programs across the U.S. It was an exciting opportunity to move to a new location and start a new program. This time, a moving van was necessary for household goods.

> These people are looking for someone with expertise to guide them in the development of their programs.

Lessons to Take Away from This Chapter:
1. Listen to mentors, individuals who have done what you do and can provide guidance.
2. Continue to learn with every experience.
3. When an opportunity drops in your lap, take it.

"Success occurs when opportunity meets preparation."
— Zig Ziglar

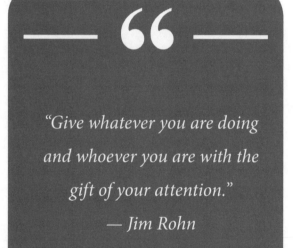

"*Give whatever you are doing
and whoever you are with the
gift of your attention.*"
— *Jim Rohn*

Chapter 4

IMPLEMENT MEDICAL EMERGENCY PROGRAMS

Portland, Oregon Life Flight

My career implementing new programs began as Chief Flight Nurse for Emanuel Life Flight, Emanuel Hospital (now Legacy Emanuel Medical Center) in Portland, Oregon in 1977. The helipad was being built on the roof of the hospital. The gracefully curved ramp was the solution to the drop from the elevated pad to the top floor entry to the hospital. My responsibilities included providing input and authority in hiring or firing, training and supervising of the flight nurses, configuring the aircraft, and writing the protocols. The crew was a pilot and one flight nurse modeled after the Denver Flight for Life Program. To cover the 12-hour shifts, we needed five nurses.

Flight nurse applicants were required to have a minimum of two years of experience in the emergency department or intensive care unit or both. Why just two years? The need was for intelligent, flexible individuals. Too long in one place or a position can cause one to become fixed on "the way we do things". Good nurses excel within a year or two on a unit. They learn quickly and become so skilled that after a year or two, they begin a quest for new experiences. They change positions or facilities to expand their knowledge and experiences. The nurses needed to be coachable and teachable.

Too long in one place or a position can cause one to become fixed on "the way we do things."

Physical requirements included normal weight for their height, agility, and physical ability to handle the stretcher, equipment, and work in the confined space of the helicopter. They needed public relationship skills to represent and present the new Life Flight Program to the community.

Emanuel Hospital leased the same type of helicopter that had been used in Denver—the Aérospatiale Alouette III. Helicopter leasing companies provided the aircraft and pilot coverage. During this time in the 1970s, there were many excellent helicopter pilots, out of the military from Vietnam and Korea, available for service.

My responsibilities included finding, selecting, buying, and configuring the medical cases. As in Denver, my sewing skills came in handy to make custom pockets for palates that fit in the medical cases to hold the ampules and syringes. I wrote the first draft of protocols and procedures for the nurses as well as the dispatch center while planning and construction progressed. Protocols were much like those at St. Anthony's. Using Denver as a model, we made modifications to suit our needs.

Shortly after my arrival in the late fall, an unexpected snow storm dumped snow on Portland. Have you ever just moved somewhere and the locals say the type of weather (usually adverse weather) is not the norm for the area? Dutifully, I carefully made my way to work to find that most people had stayed home.

One day, I became a patient at the hospital. Salmonella food poisoning, after eating at a local deli, landed me in the hospital to receive antibiotics and fluids. My medical director swore I was on the verge of death but it hadn't felt life-threatening to me. Unable to care for patients until cleared by lab tests negative of salmonella, I was dubbed "Typhoid Mary".

Shortly after we hired our nurses, we received word that a nurse had filed a suit against the program for not hiring her. They say that everyone gets sued sooner or later in our litigious society. This was an unexpected, anxiety-producing situation. Who sued for a missed position? Nervous, not knowing what to expect before the meeting, I was reminded that events are not as bad as our imagination. Staying in the moment controls the imagination that wants to live in the imagined future. We explained the candidate requirements and how we had selected staff. The committee listened carefully to all participants.

The nurse brought suit because she felt she was more qualified than any of the nurses hired. She had more than eight years of intensive care experience. The flight nurse job required an excellent clinician, a tactful and courteous manner, and public relations skills. She did not demonstrate these qualities and was declined a position by the arbitration committee. Because our decisions and choices were based on clearly defined requirements and sound observations, our decisions were upheld.

Later, we were informed this nurse experienced sudden death due to a brain aneurysm which had affected her judgment and behavior. It was fortunate she was not a flight nurse aboard a flight when it happened. God works in mysterious ways.

> Staying in the moment controls the imagination that wants to live in the imagined future.

After a disappointing attempt to have a uniform company make our flight suits, I decided to sew the two uniforms for each nurse. I made my own flight suits in Denver and designed pockets with a strap to secure scissors and the oxygen key. Gores in the calf pockets allowed extra room for bulky stethoscopes. My sister Betty and her friend actually made most of the uniforms to free up my time. The short boxy jacket and flight pants of navy blue looked sharp.

Everything came together. The nurses were trained, the dispatch set up, and the program began.

Before our rooftop helipad was completed, we used a ground level pad near the hospital. Power wires bordered the helipad. Lift off was vertical since we needed to clear the wires before forward speed. Once, just as we were lifted off to attend a PR trip, smoke started curling out of the console. I looked at the pilot who was fixed on the control gauges and working the collective and pedals. It seemed like a long time but surely it was only seconds. Time slowed as I considered my options. Should I radio in to let dispatch know there was smoke; were we going down?

> Time slowed as I considered my options. Should I radio in to let dispatch know there was smoke; were we going down?

Mayday! Were we clear of the wires? Were we going to get caught on the wires as we plummet and flip upside-down? I released the mike transmit button having said nothing aloud. It was better left unsaid. I looked about as we dropped from the sky to land hard on the on-ramp to the Fremont Bridge.

Lesson: Sometimes things are better left unsaid. The call would have been recorded. It would not be played on the evening news.

I took cues from the pilot. As soon as the blades stopped rotating, it was safe to exit the craft. We were out. We weren't sure if there would be fire where the smoke had been. The impact had broken the nose gear and there was a wrinkle in the tail boom where it attached to the body of the aircraft. As I stopped shaking, the pilot was ecstatic that the main rotor blades, although close to the ground where the nose gear collapsed, had not been damaged! My luck was still holding. No injury and, luckily, no patient. It was an engine failure.

We completed a few flights and continued with orientation drills with local fire departments. One sunny day, we were conducting a drill and orientation at a wooded site near a river. In the Alouette III, the nurse faces rearward on a bench seat in the front left of the aircraft. We had taken off and the pilot was flying over water between river banks covered with trees and foliage. When I twisted around to watch where we were going, I noticed the approach of wires stretched across the river.

> If I am to be decapitated by wires, I want it to be from the back to the front, so I turned back to face the rear of the aircraft.

"There are wires!" I exclaimed over the intercom radio. "We're going to hit!" Again time slowed and I considered the situation.

The pilot said, "No, I don't see any."

I did see wires and concluded: If I am to be decapitated by wires, I want it to be from the back to the front, so I turned back to face the rear of the aircraft. A small vibration was felt as we hit the wires. My head was still attached. We landed safely on the river bank where the inspection revealed damage to the parts of the main rotor head and rotor blades.

Fortunately, the lead pilot, who had come along for the drill, helped me convince the pilot that it was not safe to fly the aircraft out. The duty pilot felt that the damage "wasn't that bad" and he could probably fly it. Why take a chance? Everyone was safe. I was relieved when the final decision was to ground the aircraft. We waited for emergency parts and a mechanic to come and repair the aircraft. That rotor blade change was such an excellent job; I never felt such a smooth ride.

An exploration of the area revealed a telephone wire, which was not easily seen since the supporting poles had been covered by foliage. Pilots often look for poles to alert them that wires may stretch between them. The usual flight path is over the top of the poles to avoid invisible wires.

During this little trip in the woods, I found poison oak. The oils from the plant got on my jumpsuit. An itchy, blistering, burning rash spread along the backs of my legs. My sympathy for little sister Judy and her experience with poison ivy as a child bloomed.

My aircraft adventures weren't quite over. One cloudy day, we were returning to base when the cloud cover quickly moved in on us. No horizon, no ground, we were surrounded by fog. This was bad since we flew by visual flight rules. We could not see to avoid obstacles. Pilot Bill Singer, who had more than 10,000 flight hours, spied a paved area through a small hole in the clouds. He flew down through the hole to land in a residential cul-de-sac. We were lucky to find that hole. Another medical helicopter emergency landing story for the newspapers! The helicopter was flown out the next day as soon as the fog lifted.

Selling helicopter transport was difficult in the implementation years of these programs. Everyone wanted to argue the benefits and wanted documented proof of better medical outcomes. Our little incidents with the aircrafts and weather may not have been helpful but did display the expertise of our pilots. I never felt life-threatened in any of these events; some other person or patient always took priority. Today, helicopter transport and trauma centers are the standard of care. Multiple helicopter and fixed-wing transport programs exist in many cities and states.

> No horizon, no ground, we were surrounded by fog. This was bad since we flew by visual flight rules.

Standards for both public relations and clinical judgment were high. A flight nurse on a public relations trip removed her blouse to get some sun. She also went without the cardiac monitor on a mission to retrieve a hypothermia patient. These two critical errors in judgment occurred early on in her employment. The first incident was not professional and second was critical since hypothermic patients must be checked for cardiac activity before care. This led to the decision to terminate her.

Firing someone is a task not taken lightly. The nurse's actions signified major judgment issues and required action. My fears were worse than the actual process of the exit session. The nurse was aware of her shortcomings. We all know in our hearts when we are not where we are supposed to be. I was reminded again that being in the moment is not as bad as the imagined moment; this situation was weathered. If you find yourself in over your head, it is okay to ask for help or get out.

Nationwide Implementations

Evergreen Helicopters based in McMinnville, Oregon, leased aircraft to Life Flight. The owner decided to actively pursue the medical transport market for helicopters and fixed-wing leases. He had a fleet of aircraft and pilots, and a desire to be the vendor of the aircraft to new hospital programs. The expertise team was comprised of myself, as well as a pilot who had been active in a few programs, and my friend, flight nurse Sandi from Denver, who had started a program in Long Beach.

Our team traveled all over the United States to meet with hospitals, share our expertise, and submit bids to provide their helicopters and or fixed-wing aircraft. We assisted with programs in Danville, Pennsylvania, Iowa City, Iowa, Jacksonville, Florida, Houston, Texas, San Diego, California to name a few. Our protocol manuals were copied in more than one location. We were happy to help innovators wherever we went, whether we secured the contracts or not.

I was proud to be a part of the birth of hospital-based medical emergency helicopter and fixed-wing transport programs across the U.S. Hard work and high standards helped lay the foundations for programs still in business today. Emanuel Life Flight was the fourth program in the nation to start operation.

Phoenix, Arizona AirEvac

I accepted a position as Chief of Flight Nurse at Lincoln-Samaritan AirEvac in Phoenix, Arizona in 1980. I went from a green rain country to Arizona's desert sun country. We had consulted with AirEvac start-up a year earlier for their first helicopter. Their plan was to implement a second helicopter and dedicate two fixed-wing aircraft, and train dedicated flight crew members to cover these new aircraft.

> A fixed-wing aircraft dispatched to pick up a high-risk pregnant woman turned around to pick up a ride-along reporter.

Here I experienced controversy. A fixed-wing aircraft dispatched to pick up a high-risk pregnant woman turned around to pick up a ride-along reporter. Since both mom and baby were at risk, this was an unfortunate decision by an inexperienced nurse supervisor to turn the aircraft around. The reporter recognized a potential sensational story and the story was going to be the highlight of the local television's nightly news. As a result, the AirEvac program director was fired by the Executive Director of Good Samaritan Hospital on the TV news broadcast.

There followed a stress period, as the lawsuit filed by the fired AirEvac director went to trial. I testified for the AirEvac director and was instructed to obtain a psychiatric evaluation to prove that I wasn't nuts. Not handling stress well? A psychiatrist of my choice heard my story, declared me sane, but in a difficult situation.

John C. Lincoln Medical Center (JCL) and its medical director disassociated themselves from the program and it became Samaritan AirEvac. A new program director and medical director were put in place. By then the two helicopters and the two fixed-wing aircraft were up and running. However, my loyalties rested with the JCL personnel since they had been the visionaries to start the program. I recommended a great flight nurse to take my place and resigned. The psychiatrist thought maybe I could have stayed to work it out. Was I running from a problem? Maybe. This was a battle I did not want to fight.

Paramedic Training Phoenix Fire

Working for local nursing registries, staffing in intensive care units and emergency rooms, and part time as a flight nurse kept me busy. A Phoenix Fire Department Chief approached me one day in 1983 to ask me to assist in the development of a paramedic training program, citing my ability to implement programs. Great, another start-up! I liked to build from nothing but was not interested in revising the policy and protocols. A firefighter and I were tasked to develop protocols and set up the curriculum for the first Phoenix Fire Paramedic Program and graduate the first class.

This took approximately one year when I was approached to head up the flight nurses in a start-up consortium program in San Francisco and Walnut Creek, California. I was not sure how my name got around but I am thankful that it did. Starting programs was exciting for me.

It seemed that opportunities just came to me but most likely, they were a result of my previous experiences and possibly, recommendations. I said yes to this opportunity.

San Francisco CALSTAR

The 1984 CALSTAR—California Shock Trauma Air Rescue Program—was sponsored by several hospitals to provide the care and transport, and spread the cost of the program to several hospital participants. A program is expensive. Helicopters required one-hour maintenance per hour of flight and as with the fixed-wing aircraft, the fuel burn is gallons per hour per engine, not miles per gallon. This program model was designed to serve but not put as much financial strain on one facility.

The helicopter was based at John Muir Hospital in Walnut Creek. The crew worked 24 hours like fire fighters to staff the aircraft, a BK117 MBB twin-engine helicopter. By now, we had commercially-available uniforms and my sewing skills were not needed. The program was faced with some unusual California laws. The nurses had to be paramedics to work in the prehospital arena. This was a bit frustrating, considering the level of training of the flight nurses. You can imagine the soap box I wanted to be on given the differences in expertise. An agreement was reached. Nurses become certified as paramedics so they could work in the prehospital environment. The program soon began operation.

San Francisco! My apartment was a studio located on the panhandle of the Golden Gate Park and a short distance to Haight and Ashbury Streets. Any old hippie knows the significance of that location. The famous sister row houses that are depicted in many pictures of San Francisco were within walking distance out my back door. Parking was a difficult task in this neighborhood. My favorite spot was on the large sidewalk in front of my apartment. With no laundry facilities, I became acquainted with a Chinese laundry. It was really nice to have folded and pressed underwear.

I would jog down the Golden Gate Park to the ocean and back. It was cooler in San Francisco compared to the weather across the Bay Bridge in Walnut Creek. It was a great place with access to the giant redwoods, Carmel, downtown San Francisco, and Ghirardelli Square. There was even a subway that traveled across the bay. I would pass by Gilroy, the home of garlic. It was a pungent drive when the garlic was harvested. Everyone should take time to enjoy the Earth!

Boston MedFlight: One More Program

CALSTAR was up and running when hospital administrators from the east coast came to visit and suggested that my destiny was to start one more program in Boston. Boston MedFlight was a consortium model, which is why they were in California to examine the CALSTAR experience.

Once again I said yes. This time, I found out it was an Emanuel Hospital person who had recommended me for the job. It pays to always do your best and leave with good memories since you never know who will be looking for you in the future.

My contract was for two years, 1985-87, as Director of Flight Personnel for Boston MedFlight. I moved cross-country to Beverly, Massachusetts where I bought a very old house. I think the mortgage interest rate was in the teens. This consortium included the prestigious Massachusetts General Hospital, Boston City Hospital (now Boston Medical Center), University Hospital, and Brigham and Women's Hospital. Our main offices were located at the University Hospital. Our helicopter, also a BK117, was based at Logan Airport. Our staff, RN and paramedics worked 24-hour shifts. The program was up and running with ease, with helicopter and fixed-wing transports. Boston MedFlight was pretty much routine in its setup. I enjoyed exploring the area, and being a workaholic, I worked a part-time job in the emergency room of a small community hospital in Gloucester, Massachusetts.

> It pays to always do your best and leave with good memories since you never know who will be looking for you in the future.

My sisters and their families were able to drive from Michigan to visit. We went whale watching to see the great whales off the coast of Gloucester. The sea was smooth as glass that beautiful day. We visited the New England aquarium in downtown Boston and viewed historic places. Did you know regular coffee is served with cream and sugar? If you like black coffee, you have to speak quickly.

I was struck by the closeness of everything compared to the west. An hour's drive on a traffic-free highway could put you in a different state or two. When my sister Betty visited, we took the train to New York City. We had fun sightseeing and exploring Broadway.

On the street, we were offered free tickets to a show. Free was good. Imagine our surprise when the live show turned out to have nude actors! I remember the naked actors, but have no idea what the show was about because I was so shocked.

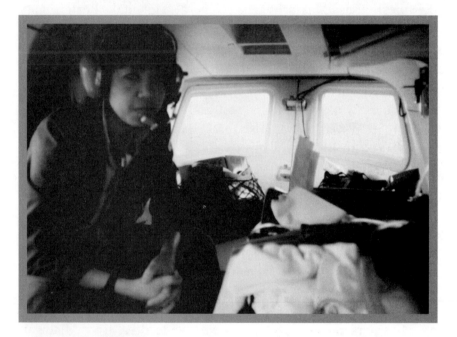

 I could not just sit back and relax at the end of my contract of two years. It was time for me to do something new. I sat in my car in stopped traffic in the right lane. A driver passing me on the right, with his right tires on the sidewalk, helped me make my decision to move. This was too crazy! Phoenix was my destination. Wide, open spaces, sunshine most every day, no ice and no snow!

My house was sold in preparation to move back to Phoenix. I rented an apartment in a converted church in Peabody, Massachusetts. I did not have a job. I had achieved my goal to start programs across the U.S. What next? This may seem to have been a little foolhardy but I knew I could work somewhere as a nurse.

> I could not just sit back and relax at the end of my contract of two years. It was time for me to do something new.

Lessons to Take Away from This Chapter:
1. Don't be afraid to make a change if you need to.
2. To master fear, one must live in the moment.
3. Some people are made to organize and start a business, others prefer daily operations and revising policies.

"Do the thing you fear most and the death of fear is certain."
—Mark Twain

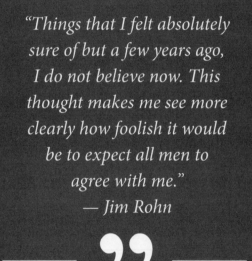

"Things that I felt absolutely sure of but a few years ago, I do not believe now. This thought makes me see more clearly how foolish it would be to expect all men to agree with me."
— Jim Rohn

Chapter 5

WRAPPING UP

Independence: Nursing Registry Shift Work

After contacting nursing registry organizations, I began working per diem in the intensive care units and emergency departments at Phoenix hospitals. Working registry requires a discipline to work when offered shifts. Proactive, I would pre-book a month in advance and would often work for a year or two in the same facility or unit. The units varied from burn unit, trauma, medical, surgical, neurology, and cardiac intensive care. My experience and skills as a flight nurse fit easily into critical care and emergency department units. Working in various units and environments was not unlike working as a flight nurse since it involved total care for one or two patients at a time and a different environment each day.

> Listen to that subconscious! It's trying to tell you something that's usually very important and usually right.

Assignments were often heavy for registry nurses. I learned to listen to my instincts when entering a new situation. Listen to that subconscious! It's trying to tell you something that's usually very important and usually right.

My routine began with overall observation and correction of potential issues prior to the start of care. Incompatible drug mixtures could be caught and rectified before too much time had elapsed.

I made my own schedule and worked my schedule. Vacation was built into the schedule. As long as I expected to work, there was no trouble getting shifts. If I started getting worried about getting hours, shifts would be cancelled. I got what I expected. Other nurses complaining about not getting shifts asked me how I was getting shifts. I explained the attitude of expectation. Working per diem, you become your own boss. If you don't schedule or you turn down every offer of work, it won't work.

A Family Start-Up

I collaborated with little brother Joe to start Modular Solutions, Ltd., The Complete Modular Building Company in 1995. Joe had seen my career with start-ups and determined my skill was needed to help him start a business. This company builds commercial factory-built buildings for school classrooms, offices, clinics or even a city hall. Less construction waste, the building and site work progressing at the same time could save customers money and shorten the time from the start to a finished installation of a building. We developed a business plan, logo, name, and a corporate structure.

> Chemotherapy pounded away at every replicating cell in my body. Pain in my hands and feet limited my abilities.

I wrote the business plan while I attended a college course on writing business plans. The instructor mentioned that very few people had ever finished a business plan by the end of their course and congratulated me. The class was the opportune time to accomplish the plan. It helped in attaining our first contracts. There were tests, licenses, and processes we needed to complete for start-up and these were done one step at a time.

A student contest at an art school developed the company logo. A description of the company's mission and products inspired the winning student to create a great logo. We set up all the processes that identified us as a company. Modular Solutions, Ltd. is a successful company today.

Overcoming Leukemia

In 1996, after pushing a patient bed up a ramp, I developed debilitating severe low back pain and spasms. A routine visit with my primary doctor revealed that this pain was a result of acute lymphocytic leukemia. Immediately hospitalized for the start of chemotherapy induced over a month, I lost 30 pounds and my hair!

Chemotherapy pounded away at every replicating cell in my body. Pain in my hands and feet limited my abilities. If I tripped, I was unable to react to save myself from a fall. A tunneled intravenous catheter was placed in my chest to allow for blood draws and administration of chemotherapy. At intervals, spinal injections of the chemotherapy was used to prevent any brain cancer. The chemo was intermittent over seven months. During the first month, I experienced some of the longest minutes of my life. Nothing is worse than being too weak to get out of bed when the bathroom is belching sewer gas—true story. That night, 12:00

midnight to 12:05 lasted two days! Yes, time was distorted. I demanded an airbed mattress so I would be able to move on the bed and be comfortable.

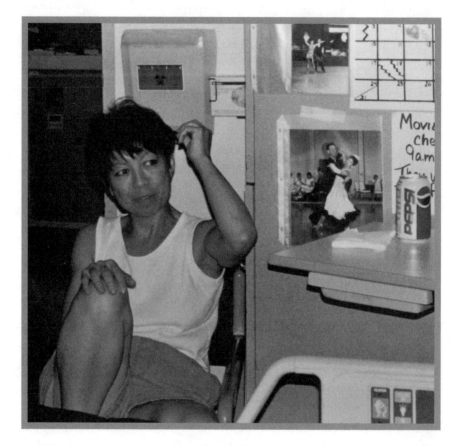

As soon as I was diagnosed, my siblings sprang into action. They came to visit and took turns staying with me during the year of chemo and recovery. They had to flush my central catheter line since my hands were not strong enough to push a syringe plunger. A credit to everyone, a line infection never occurred! Even though I could not perform the task, I could teach and observe to ensure the technique used did not lead to complications.

At first, my sisters Betty, Judy, and Beta came to my aid. When it was brother Ray's (Junior) turn, I was uncertain because it was difficult for me to get out of the bathtub. No showers were allowed with a tunneled central line in the chest. Tap water can cause infections. One doesn't parade naked in front of brothers. When this doubt was put to him, he stated, "No problem. I know how to call 911." It was so funny it ended my concern. No 911 call was necessary.

It was a time of sleepless nights, weeping, and depression for me. Listening to a special musical score by Dr. Andrew Weil was the only way to fall sleep at night. Days and nights were endless. I was tired of thinking about what to try to eat at the next meal when plagued by nausea. If it wasn't for family support and ginger syrup, I would never have made it. Wisps of remaining hair were shaved off by my hairdresser friend after most had fallen out. I crocheted and wore caps. My memories of this time were fragmented by my "chemo brain". One friend states he visited frequently. I have no memory of any visit with him.

> "No problem. I know how to call 911."

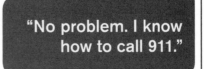

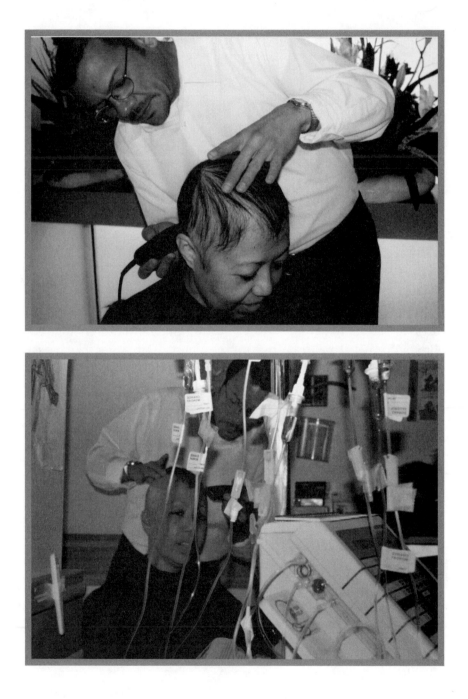

Judy would not let me sit around. We designed and sewed small beanie baby quilts for our nieces and nephews. An appliqued scenic top had pockets to house beany babies, small stuffed animal TY toys popular during that time. We made a large appliqued scenic wall hanging that was appraised at $1,200 when finished. My nephews Ray and Kris came. Kris learned to make scrub pants to wear for work. Mind and hands busy with design and sewing helped pass the time in a fun, productive way. It was purposeful in a time when time seemed aimless.

My brother Joe introduced me to ozone therapy that helped others with cancers to survive. Ozone is O_3 gas made from oxygen (O_2) by a generator. The ozone was used to augment the traditional chemotherapy. The ozone therapy involved flowing ozone gas into each ear canal twice a day for a month, then once a day thereafter. The ozone would kill cancer cells.

In the 1930s, it was thought that ozone was the cure for all cancers. Ozone is considered controversial and unproven by most mainstream medical professionals. This story is not to recommend ozone to you, but to relate what worked for me.

I spoke with other individuals who were using ozone at that time. One man had been told there was no hope and no more chemo would be offered. Since he didn't have $100,000 for a bone marrow transplant, he used the ozone therapy. He regained his strength and went back to work as an animal chiropractor. He was using only ozone and his leukemia was under control. A woman with recurrent breast cancer stated that she was feeling great, using the ozone and taking the traditional chemo.

Of the three of newly-diagnosed leukemia patients treated by my oncologist at the time, I was the only survivor.

While dealing with cancer, I explored alternative ways to get better even though I was sure the chemo was killing me. Contradictory thoughts, I know. I read books on natural cures and juiced foods for better nutrition. An unfortunate woman whose whole family was on HIV medications once told me that high-fat foods held nausea caused by meds at bay. My stock meal became bacon, eggs, and buttered toast. It was easy to weep and feel sorry but sewing was a great help. I was well enough to return to work almost one year to the date of diagnosis. I am cured!

Taking Control

In 2001, all my retirement funds in the stock market were lost as someone else controlled my money. It was a hard lesson. No one cares about your money like you do. I spent thousands paying capital gains taxes on money that was gone. I resolved to learn more about financial management and take control of my finances. Most recently, Tony Robbins' book, *Money: Master the Game*, has proved most informative. There are resources available to learn more about preserving hard-earned money.

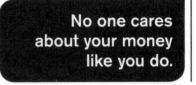

No one cares about your money like you do.

In 2002, I was diagnosed with dilated cardiomyopathy as manifested by extreme shortness of breath on exertion and coughing, which led to a short time off. My heart was pumping at 15% of its capability. This condition was either a result of the chemotherapy or from the Agent Orange exposure in Vietnam. This was reversed by drug therapy. Experiencing extreme shortness of breath is a frightening experience. Delaying care until this developed is not the best idea I ever had. Medications to remove fluid and strengthen my heart muscle proved effective. When you know something is wrong with your health, don't be stubborn—seek medical attention.

In 2008, the climate for registry work changed as hospitals advertised they would no longer use registry nurses. This had happened in the past, but now graduate nurses who were promised positions were fired. Sensing this change would impact my ability to work, I obtained a position in the Veterans Administration (VA) Hospital intensive care unit (ICU), and soon after, was transferred to nuclear medicine to administer heart stress tests. The acuity of the ICU patients in a non-trauma facility did not hold my interest. Performing one potentially very interesting heart stress test at a time was more to my liking.

My responsibilities included all aspects of the procedure from evaluating consults to calling to schedule and administering the stress portion of the tests. As the sole RN in nuclear medicine, my responsibilities also included teaching new technicians how to insert intravenous catheters, assisting with assessment of ill patients, and helping to develop order sets to assist with new PET/CT scan instructions and orders. I wrote a manual of the protocols and procedures for all the tasks I was performing. My orientation for a week was by word of mouth. Future staff training would not be the experience as mine had been. Passing information by word of mouth ends up much like the game of gossip, operating on perceived rules and missing details. My goal was to have written policies which supported the standard operating procedures. Several revisions of the policies were made as things changed, something I swore never to do!

> Wishing doesn't always work, most goals will take some action step on your part.

Most recently, my job is reviewing consults and coordination of medical appointments not offered by the VA. Full circle for most consults are for eye care! I am able to perform this job from home, working on a secure computer network. I prepared a vision board a few years back and on it was "work at home!" A vision board has pictures depicting things you would like in your life such as a car, house, or travel. I did have to take action and apply for a position that could be done from home. Wishing doesn't always work, most goals will take some action step on your part.

According to the Gallup polls, ranking professions on honesty and ethical standards, nurses have ranked as the most trusted for years. I have attempted to maintain the highest of standards and

deliver the best care possible to my patients. Even in personal high-risk situations, the patient's needs became my priority. Outstanding individuals with their high standards and pursuit of excellence helped hone my skills and abilities to the highest level. In turn, I expected above average performance from those round me. It is proven that high expectations result in individuals performing better.

In seeking ongoing knowledge, I found the process of learning most interesting.

Four Stages of Learning Can Be Recognized:
1. Unconscious incompetence: You don't know what you don't know.
2. Conscious incompetence: You know you don't know. This is where just about everybody quits.
3. Conscious competence: You can perform but must think of every step.
4. Unconscious competence: You perform without thinking.

I recognize these stages in each new complex endeavor and teach it to students. The trick is to keep on trying until action is an unconscious competent act. Do you remember your last drive home? No? That was an unconscious competent act.

In my lifetime, I have seen the recognition of what our Declaration of Independence said long ago—all men are created equal. It's still a hard nut to crack, since prejudices seem to shift.

In my life, the hardest thing I have found to do is the ability to rely on other people. Growing up, I had learned to become self-reliant and independent. I learned a lot about teamwork and the benefits of review as a flight nurse. Learning and working on self-development as head of a group session, I noted arguing for limitations led to failure. A woman kept insisting, "I can't, I can't." She couldn't and didn't do the task everyone else had done, until she gave up, saying "I can't".

"Argue for your limitations and sure enough they are yours."
—Richard Bach

At a boot camp, our group success depended on individuals working together and assisting each other. This camp was a physical and mental challenge. I learned there is a time to give up fear, ask for help if needed, live in the moment, and accomplish extraordinary things. As I walked briskly across a long bed of red hot coals—my feet not burning—I was impressed. Amazing what one can do if you believe in yourself, follow instructions, and learn from others. Don't be an idiot and walk slowly through a bed of hot coals.

My high school goals were met. As a nurse I participated in a war, visited exotic locations, traveled the U.S. starting new helicopter transport programs, and made some money. Vacations have taken me to great locations. In the past few years, finally there's been a "thank you for your service" as citizens recognized military veterans and active duty soldiers. Hobbies have developed my artistic talents. As I continue to learn new things every day, maybe it's time to write new goals.

Lessons to Take Away from This Chapter

1. What holds you back may not be your beliefs but some influence of family, peers, or the media.
2. The past does not dictate the future.
3. Continuous growth is the key to success.
4. No one cares about your money like you do.
5. Don't worry about what other people think because they are probably thinking about themselves.
6. What you expect often determines what you get.

P.S.: My house has 2.5 baths.

~~∞∞∞~~

"Anything worth doing is worth doing poorly—
until you can learn to do it well."
— Zig Ziglar

~~∞∞∞~~

‹ ‹

Scan the code for a FREE downloadable
copy of *Tough Lessons* and learn how to
manage turbulence in your life now!
www.toughlessons.net

What Other People
Say about Mary Hart

"She is a survivor! She is a risk-taker. When I asked her why be in Toastmasters, she answered, 'For self-improvement'. 'If you think you have something to say, better learn how to say it.' Mary has high expectations and standards for herself and expects quality work from workers around her. If Mary were in grade school now, she would have been identified as gifted and placed in programs that would have helped her to develop academic skills as well to help her to believe in herself."

—Betty Hart, Aiea High School retired teacher, sister

"I can tell many stories about Mary. Mary can accomplish anything she puts her mind to, no matter what it is."

—Ray L. Hart, Jr., brother

"Mary was always just my sister Mary until I was asked to write about her. I realized that she would do exactly what she wanted to do and when she wanted to do it. Why? Because she and she alone made it happen. I was happy to be entrusted with her car when she went to Vietnam. I am not sure she realized that I was a pushover when it came to lending out the hot rod Camaro!"

—Beta Cook, entrepreneur, Rusty Nail Restaurant, sister

"My sister Mary Hart is someone to look up to. She is creative, artistic, and can visualize things. She is giving. She has high energy. She works hard. She is vocal. And she is opinionated."

—Judy Young, charity worker, sister

"As long as I can remember, Mary has been one of the best people I know. You could say she's a Girl Scout (the oath). Growing up, she always had an encouraging word to everyone, always had a positive spin to everything. Mary excelled at everything she has done. Mary is not afraid of high risks. From serving in Vietnam to investing in stocks, her risk level is way above the average. Her loyalty to family is beyond reproach. Being her little brother, I know that better then everyone on the planet."

—Joe Hart, entrepreneur, Modular Solutions, Ltd., brother

"Ms. Hart is an articulate, erudite perfectionist. She specializes in clarity in her actions. This carries over to her communication skills. Her book should make for an interesting journey. Expect from Ms. Hart's writing what you experience in person. No-nonsense, straight talk, articulate, accurate. In other words, cut to the chase and don't baffle me with poppycock (boushwah)."

—Ed Goldstein, MD, nuclear radiologist

"Characteristics of Mary include, strong ethics, hard worker, determined, self-sacrificing for others, wise, knowledgeable, well-versed, and well-traveled, a loving family member, a caring friend, and a humble person. Mary never brags or boasts about her adventures in life. The truth is, one has to pry it out of her. I can only imagine what other journeys she has been on and survived that the world knows nothing about."

—Stacy O'Neall, nuclear technician

"Mary has endured and embraced all the good and evil this world has to offer and is still, always, willing to go the extra mile for those around her. Her lineage won't be based on a blood line, but on the knowledge she's bestowed on everyone she encounters. If I needed to simply sum Mary up, I could say that she is, truly, one of a kind."

—Chad Stoddard, nuclear technician

"Mary has the ability to make complex concepts understandable for everyone, whether it's the demonstration of blood flow with her hands as models, to making the best pickles I have ever had. I sometimes joke that if I were sick and needed a nurse that would not let me get away with feeling sorry for myself, I would want Mary because I would be on my feet in no time."

—Sheila Smith, nuclear technician

"Mary is a methodic, rational person who keeps you in a good prospective view of things. She is a really smart person. She loves to read and goes to trainings to learn more and more. It's like she doesn't get tired of learning. A long time ago, I told her that she should go back to school to get a master's degree. To tell you the truth, her knowledge is like she has a PhD. Mary is an excellent, caring nurse and an amazing person who is a real pleasure to work with. I am looking forward to working by her side for more years and learning from her."

—Carol Rodriquez, RN

"Aunt Mary has been a nurse for as long as I have known her. She has overcome many challenges and nothing holds her back. The projects she takes on, she completes. She is the type of woman who is continuously trying to better herself."

—Leilani Hart, niece

Resources

More Information about the Helicopter Transport Programs May Be Found on the Internet Links Below:

Flight For Life® Colorado - Air Medical Transport across the Rocky Mountain Region, www.flightforlifecolorado.org.

Emanuel Life Flight - The first hospital-based air ambulance in the West coast, the 4th in the nation, www.lifeflight.org/about/history.

Air Evac - wholly-owned subsidiary of PHI Air Medical, provides services across Arizona, U.S., Canada and Mexico, www.phicares.com/states/arizona.

CALSTAR - Support is provided by hospitals as well as corporate, foundations, and individual contributors, www.calstar.org.

Boston MedFlight - A critical care air and ground transport system for critically ill and injured patients in the region, www.bostonmedflight.org/history.

References:

Executive Directors Report, "The Most Trusted Profession… Where Do You Fit In? Nurses Are #1 Again!," *ARIZONA NURSE,* February/March/April 2016, page 8.

Robbins, Tony. *MONEY Master The Game: 7 Simple Steps to Financial Freedom* (New York: Simon & Schuster, 2014).

MARY HART
Author – Speaker - Trainer
info@toughlessons.net

....

Mary Hart

Independent World Ventures Representative

www.travelwithhart.rovia.com

Book Travel

www.travelwithhart.worldventures.biz

www.travelwithhart.dreamstrips.com

....

Member Woodland Native People
www.woodlandnativepeople.com

....

OnSite Construction Management LLC

www.onsitecm.com

We assist in all phases of construction and take pride in
turnkey building development. OnSite offers a variety of
building options for custom design of
commercial modular buildings.

Mary Hart, President

- Email: estimating@onsitecm.com
- Phone: 602-402-6321 * Fax: 602-237-8471
- Mail: PO Box 5167 Phoenix, AZ 85010

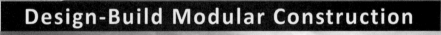
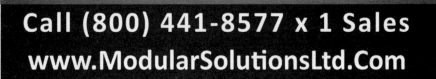

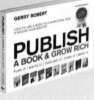

OTHER BOOKS RECOMMENDED BY BLACK CARD BOOKS

The Financial Toolbox
Your Best Business Guide To:
Less Tax, Greater Profit And
More Time!
Jessie Christo

From Empty To
Empowered
The Power Of Pets:
A Journey To Healing
From Unexpected Pet Loss
Marybeth Haines

The Marriage Code Book
Premarital & Marital
Strategies
Jack Mamo

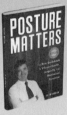

Posture Matters
The New Guidebook To
Vibrant Health, Longevity,
And Maximized Potential
Dr. Tim Errington

An Engaged Workforce
6 Practical Steps To Creating
A Coaching Culture
Mariam Sha, PhD

Put An End To Fear
New Security Solutions
For South Africa
Gregory Jurrius

Client Satisfaction 2.0
10 Powerful Strategies
To Rule The World Of
Client Servicing
V. Prema And V. Natarajan

The Art of Money
How To Win
The Wealth Game
Dr. Daleen Smal

www.blackcardbooks.com

OTHER BOOKS RECOMMENDED BY BLACK CARD BOOKS

Cloud Agent
*How Real Estate Can Combine
Cloud Technology With A
Powerful Mindset To Produce
Extraordinary Results*
Derrick Ruiz

**How To Buy Or Sell A
Home Without Getting
Screwed!**
*Buy Right, Sell Right, Reduce
Stress, And Stay Sane!*
Jason C. Campbell

**Holistic Dimensions
Of Wealth**
It Is Not Just About Money
Alexey Medvedev

The D.K.D. Principle
*10 Steps To Massively Maintain
And Retain Black Hair*
Caleta Wright and
Shontice Morris

Master The Art Of Life
*A 21-Day Journey From
Zero To Hero*
Anh Thu Nguyen &
Simone Micheletti

Wellness, The New Luxury
*A Modern Paradigm
To Truly Having It All!*
Sally May Tan

Be Heard
*Raise Your Brand's Mindshare
In Multicultural Communities*
Shilpa Gauba

**Charge Up Your
Organisation**
*Getting Real About Company
'Diss-ease' And Its Sickening
Effect On Profitability*
Ashikka Mooloo Veerasamy

POWERED BY

www.blackcardbooks.com